WHAT · DO · WE · KNOW ABOUT PREHISTORIC PEOPLE?

MIKE CORBISHLEY

PETER BEDRICK BOOKS
NEW YORK

Published by
Peter Bedrick Books
2112 Broadway
New York, NY 10023

Text © Mike Corbishley 1994

Published by agreement with Macdonald Young Books, England

Library of Congress Cataloging-in-Publication Data
Corbishley, Mike.
    What do we know about Prehistoric people? / Mike Corbishley.
        p.   cm.
    Includes index.
    ISBN 0-87226-383-5
    1. Man, Prehistoric—Juvenile literature.   I. Title.
GN744.C64   1995
930.1—dc20   95-11224
                                                     CIP
                                                      AC

Design: David West
               Children's Book Design

Illustrator: Ian Thompson

Commissioning editor: Debbie Fox

Copy editor: Jayne Booth

Picture research: Val Mulcahy

Photograph acknowledgements:
Cover front and back: The Ancient Art & Architecture Collection
(L. Ellison); The Ancient Art & Architecture Collection, p27(tl), p43(b)
(Mike Andrew); Ashmolean Museum, Oxford, p20(l); The Trustees of the
British Museum, p13(c), p13(t), p24(r), p30, p32(b); Butser Ancient Farm
Project Trust, p14, p15; Cambridge University Museum of Archaeology
and Anthropology, p27(tr), p37(t), p37(c); J. Allan Cash Photolibrary, p18,
p43(tl); Sue Cunningham/Sue Cunningham Photographic, p42; English
Heritage Photo Library, p23, p26/27, p40; Giraudon, p16(r), p17(l); Robert
Harding Picture Library, p20(r), p21(bl), p31(b) (Dr Pfirrmann), p34,
p36(b); Magnum, p16(l) (Steve McCurry), p17(r) (Thomas Hoepker),
p18/19 (Ernst Haas), p32/33 (Rene Burri); Milwaukee Public Museum,
USA, p8(l); Museum of London, p12, p12/13, p14/15, p22/23(t), p40/41;
The Museum of the Wiltshire Archaeological and Natural History Society,
Devizes, p31(c); National Museum of Greenland, p25; National Museum
of Ireland, Dublin, p35(b), p36(t); Natural history Museum, London,
p28(r); Office of Public Works, Ireland, p32(t); Phoebe Hearst Museum of
Anthropology, The University of California at Berkeley, p29, p35(t);
Picturepoint, p19, p22/23(b), p27(b), p31(t), p43(tr), Salisbury and South
Wiltshire Museum, p8(r), p37(b) (English Heritage Photo Library);
Somerset Levels Project, p38 (Dr J.M. Coles); Roger Vlitos, p32(c);
Werner Foreman Archive: p9 and p39 Field Museum of Natural History,
Chicago, p21(c) and p21(cr) British Museum, London, p22 Auckland
Institute and Museum, Auckland, p24(l) Soc. Polymathique du Morbihan,
p28(l) Centennial Museum, Vancouver, p38/39 Museum Fur Volkerkunde,
Berlin, p41 Hermitage Museum, Leningrad; Zefa, endpapers.

Typeset by: Goodfellow & Egan, Cambridge

Printed and bound in Hong Kong: by Wing King Tong Co., Ltd.

Cover photography: Tollund Man – the well-preserved remains of a
man from Tollund, Denmark, who was sacrificed around 200 BC
(see page 15).

Endpapers: Enormous statues made about AD 1000 by the people of Easter
Island in the Pacific Ocean (see page 27).

99 98 97 96 95   1 2 3 4 5

· CONTENTS ·

· W H O · · W E R E · PREHISTORIC · P E O P L E ?

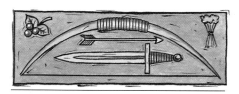

You have probably come across the word history or historic before. Adding the letters pre- to a word simply means 'before'. Prehistoric is the word archaeologists use for the period of time in the past before people discovered how to write. Once writing had been invented, there were records of what had happened in the past. This is called history. Different people started making written records at different periods around the world. The earliest writing was invented by the Sumerians in the Near East around 3250 BC. There are still some peoples who live today the way their ancestors did.

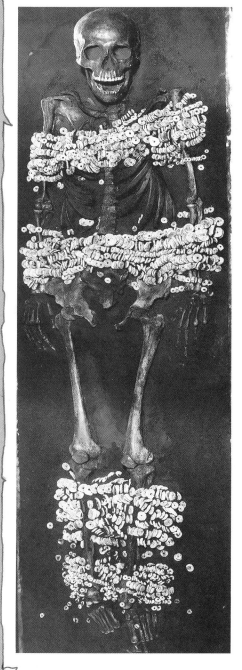

FINDING THE EVIDENCE
We can find out about the past from both the objects and the writings people leave behind. The only evidence we have for the millions of years of prehistoric times are the objects. These might be clothes or tools or paintings, or even whole buildings. We call these objects archaeological evidence. This is a photograph (left) of the skeleton of a young woman who was buried about AD 1200 in present-day Wisconsin. Although most of what she was buried with has rotted away, archaeologists do have some clues to work with. She must have been an important person, perhaps even a princess, because she has hundreds of shell beads as decoration around her shoulders, waist and legs. Shells were considered valuable by these people.

Early human sites

● Early human sites

▨ Domestication of plants and animals

☐ Extent of ice sheet 20,000 BC

Archaeologists have to be very careful when they uncover the evidence for the past. Not everything survives. Archaeologists have to work like police detectives uncovering the clues and making detailed records of them. Then they can try to work out what it all means. This man (left) was buried in a hole cut into the chalk in southern England around 2000 BC. His body must have been dressed but the clothes have rotted. He was carefully arranged, as you can see, holding a drinking pot in his hands. Perhaps this was for nourishment on his journey to the next world. By his left arm, resting on a stone, is his dagger. The handle has rotted but the bronze blade survives.

THE DEVELOPMENT OF THE FIRST PEOPLE

Human beings have been around for a lot longer than most people think! Between 10 million and 4 million years ago a type of early human being (called a *hominid*) developed in Africa. This type was called *Australopithecus*. Archae-ologists have even found the actual footprints of one of these people from 3.4 million years ago! Another early type of human, called *Homo,* also came from Africa around 2.5 million years ago. This type was called *Homo habilis* and *Homo erectus*. The remains of *Homo erectus* were found later in other parts of the world – in China and East Asia. Some of our own species, *Homo sapiens,* lived in Europe from about 400,000 to about 200,000 years ago. These early hunters were called *Homo sapiens neanderthalensis*. The earliest evidence for *Homo sapiens sapiens* – that is modern humans – is from 100,000 years ago.

CLEVER PEOPLE

Prehistoric people were skilled in many ways. This bird, either a raven or a crow, was cut from a piece of copper and has a pearl for an eye. It was made by someone from a prehistoric farming community in present-day Ohio, around 100 BC.

TIMELINE

	BC 900,000 -100,000	100,000-8000	8000-5000	5000-0	
AFRICA	100,000 First evidence of modern people *homo sapiens sapiens* in eastern and southern Africa.	10,000 Hunting camps in Sahara region after last Ice Age. 8500 First rock art in the Sahara region.	6500 Domesticated cattle in Africa. 6000 Wheat and barley first domesticated in north-eastern Africa.	4000 Millet and sorghum cultivated in the Sudan.	
				Flints	
ASIA, CHINA AND AUSTRALASIA	900,000 Earliest hominids in western Asia. 450,000 Earliest evidence for humans in China. 120,000 *Homo sapiens* type in Java. 120,000 Neanderthal peoples in western Asia. First discovered burials.	25,000 First human settlers in Australia. 9000 First wheat harvested in Syria. First sheep domesticated in Mesopotamia.	8000 First true farming community at Jericho. More islands created in south-east Asia at end of the Ice Age. 7000 Wheat and barley cultivated in Anatolia. Pig domesticated in Anatolia. 6000 First farming villages in China.	4500 Farming established around River Ganges, India. 1500 First 'writing' in China.	
EUROPE	850,000 Earliest hominids reach Europe from Africa. 600,000 First handaxes in use. 300,000 Lakeside hunters' settlements in Germany. 120,000 Neanderthal peoples are. first humans to bury their dead.	40,000 Last Ice Age. 35,000 First modern humans in Europe. 30,000 First cave art. 8300 Glaciers retreat. Hunting techniques change and stone tools become smaller and more sophisticated.	6500 First farmers in the Balkans. 6500 Britain separated from mainland Europe by melting of ice. 6200 Farming villages in western Mediterranean. 5200 Farming spreads as far as the Netherlands.	4500 Megalithic tombs in western Europe. 4000 Flint mines. 4000 First farmers in Britain still using stone tools. 3500 Simple plows first used in northern and western Europe. 3200 Circles of megalithic stones in Britain and northern France.	
AMERICAS	**North American hut**	30,000 People first reach Alaska. 20,000 Hunters moving south across North America. 12,000 People first reach Mesoamerica. 10,000 People reach the southern tip of South America.	8000 New types of stone tools. Most big game animals die out. First burials. 7000 First crops cultivated in Mexico. Some semi-permanent farming settlements in North America. 6300 Grain and potato cultivation in Peru.	5000 Cultivation of maize in Mexico. Small-scale cultivation in Amazon region. 4000-3000 Inuits (Eskimos) moved from Asia into America. 1200 First civilizations in Mesoamerica.	

10

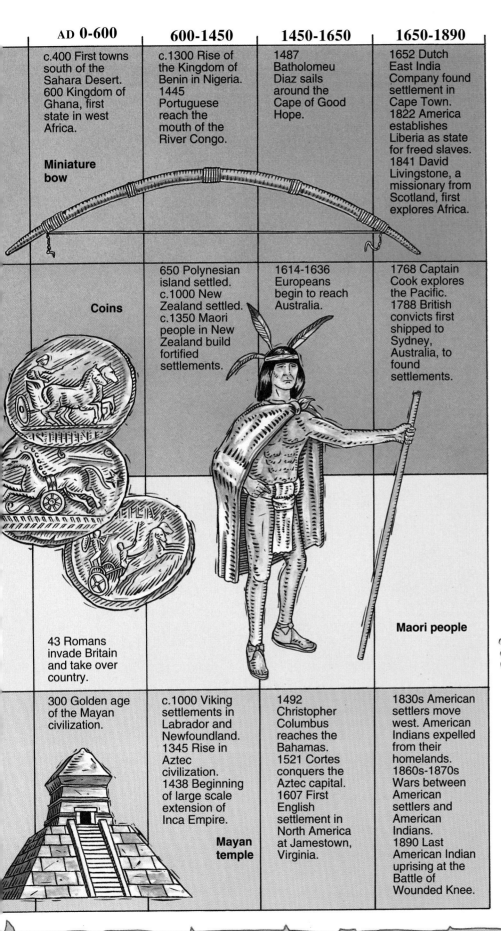

AD 0-600	600-1450	1450-1650	1650-1890
c.400 First towns south of the Sahara Desert. 600 Kingdom of Ghana, first state in west Africa. **Miniature bow**	c.1300 Rise of the Kingdom of Benin in Nigeria. 1445 Portuguese reach the mouth of the River Congo.	1487 Batholomeu Diaz sails around the Cape of Good Hope.	1652 Dutch East India Company found settlement in Cape Town. 1822 America establishes Liberia as state for freed slaves. 1841 David Livingstone, a missionary from Scotland, first explores Africa.
Coins 43 Romans invade Britain and take over country.	650 Polynesian island settled. c.1000 New Zealand settled. c.1350 Maori people in New Zealand build fortified settlements.	1614-1636 Europeans begin to reach Australia.	1768 Captain Cook explores the Pacific. 1788 British convicts first shipped to Sydney, Australia, to found settlements. **Maori people**
300 Golden age of the Mayan civilization. **Mayan temple**	c.1000 Viking settlements in Labrador and Newfoundland. 1345 Rise in Aztec civilization. 1438 Beginning of large scale extension of Inca Empire.	1492 Christopher Columbus reaches the Bahamas. 1521 Cortes conquers the Aztec capital. 1607 First English settlement in North America at Jamestown, Virginia.	1830s American settlers move west. American Indians expelled from their homelands. 1860s-1870s Wars between American settlers and American Indians. 1890 Last American Indian uprising at the Battle of Wounded Knee.

PREHISTORIC NOT PRIMITIVE

Sometimes you hear people say that something is 'prehistoric'. What they mean is that it is so out-of-date it is primitive. Throughout this book you will find that prehistoric people were not primitive. They simply lived in ways which were very different from the way of life many of us have today. Prehistoric peoples were not the same all over the world. Over the centuries in some areas, people moved from a hunting existence to farming and living in towns. In other places people lived peacefully with their environment, taking only what they needed – a way of life many modern people are just beginning to appreciate. You also need to understand that we cannot know everything about prehistoric peoples. Because they did not leave any writing describing what was happening, we often have to make guesses about what they did or meant using the evidence that survives.

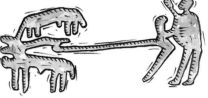

BC or AD?

Our dates are taken from the year Christ was born. The letters AD stand for Anno Domini which means 'in the year of the Lord'. The years before Christ (BC) are counted backwards. Some of prehistory stretches so far back into the past that we also talk about so many thousands, or even millions, of years ago.

11

· D I D · PREHISTORIC PEOPLE EAT · W E L L ? ·

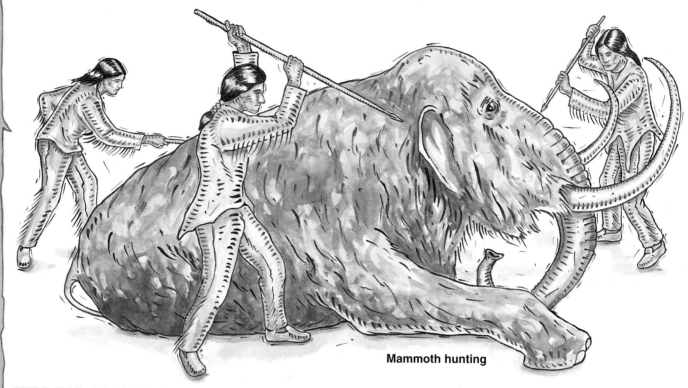

The first peoples had to find their own food to survive. We call these people hunter-gatherers because they had to hunt animals, fish and gather food. These people ate well if there was enough food to hunt and collect. Early prehistoric peoples had to know where the animals would go for water. They became experts at finding out where tasty plants and roots grew. Many Aborigines of Australia still hunt and gather their food today. Different animals and plants provided food for people all over the world. Some peoples still hunted after they started farming (see page 14).

Mammoth hunting

KILLING A MAMMOTH

The hunters above lived in North America about 9000 BC. They depended on a variety of animals and plants for food. The huge animal is a mammoth but the people also hunted bison, horses and tapirs. They have driven the mammoth into a ravine and are attacking it with stone-tipped spears. The animal's flesh will provide plenty of food for this hunting group – probably 25 to 50 people.

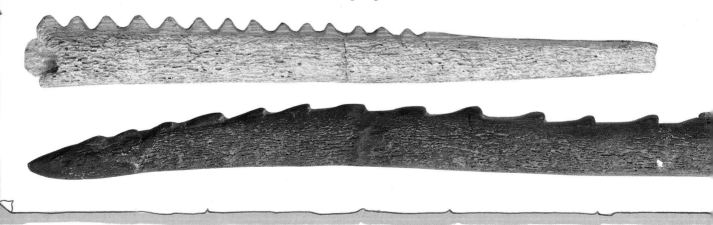

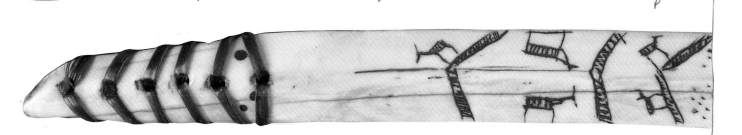

ARCTIC HUNTERS

The Inuit and other hunting peoples of the Arctic decorated ivory tools like this one above. It is a knife made from walrus ivory and it was used to cut blocks of ice to make an *igloo,* which is an Inuit house. Ivory and animal bone were used to make tools and weapons. The Inuit hunted animals such as seals, reindeer and caribou across the ice. They used *kayaks* – fast-moving canoes made of animal skins – for hunting sea birds as well as for fishing.

SWIMMING REINDEER

This picture of two swimming reindeer (below) was carved onto the tip of a mammoth's tusk around 10,500 BC. It was found in a rock shelter (see page 18) overlooking a river in south-western France. The hunting groups at this time in northern Europe followed the great herds of animals such as reindeer and relied on them for food. Their skins and bones were used to make tools and weapons.

HUNTING WEAPONS

Hunters invented different weapons to kill and catch their food. Flint was a favorite material for making sharp points for arrows and spears. But the hunters also used bone, ivory, antler and wood. You can see the remains of two hunting weapons below on the left. The top one is the point of a harpoon for spearing fish. It was carved out of antler about 10,000 years ago. The barbs would stick in the flesh of the fish. The one below is similar but has been put onto a new wooden shaft.

COLLECTING FOOD

Large quantities of food were collected, rather than hunted, by prehistoric peoples. Some of the foods collected were:
edible roots
wild barley and oats
plants like nettles
all sorts of nuts
small animals like lizards
honey
We know that people fished. This illustration (left) is of a rock engraving from Sweden. Can you see the anchor and two fishing lines?

WHO GREW FOOD·IN PREHISTORIC ·TIMES?·

In about 10,000 BC in the countries we now call Iran, Iraq, Turkey, Jordan and Israel, the climate changed. The great ice sheets had melted and there was more rain. This new climate produced woodland and wild grasses. People here gradually discovered they could save and replant the seeds of these wild grasses. Elsewhere, prehistoric hunters became farmers at different times. Wild grasses and beans were first cultivated in Peru in about 8300 BC. Crops were first grown in Mexico and root vegetables cultivated in New Guinea in 7000 BC. By 6000 BC there were farming villages in China.

PLANTING THE CROPS

After the Ice Age in Europe and Asia, the farmers' first job was to clear land to plant the crops. Seeds were scattered by hand over the cleared land. The world's first cultivated seeds were two types of wheat, called einkorn and emmer. Barley was also grown. In about 5000 BC, people in the area of America around Mexico discovered how to replant wild maize (often called corn cob). The maize was ground into flour and also used to make beer. Prehistoric peoples in different parts of the world grew all sorts of crops – millet, soy beans and rice in China, potatoes in the Andes and sorghum in Africa, for example.

PLOWING THE FIELDS

Some prehistoric peoples discovered how to plow up land before planting their crops. The first evidence comes from Mesopotamia around 4500 BC. Above, people are recreating a type of plowing used in prehistoric Britain. Two cows are pulling a wooden plow. On the right are copies of rock carvings from prehistoric Sweden. Can you see the farmer and animals?

Plowing

We have some extraordinary evidence of prehistoric people's food from the remains preserved inside the stomach of a man who was killed around 200 BC in Tollund, Denmark. He was probably sacrificed by being hanged and then thrown into a peat bog. The waterlogged peat helped to preserve his body and his clothes. Because his body was so well preserved, archaeologists were able to find the remains of his last meal. He had eaten a sort of gruel or porridge made from barley and linseed mixed with some weeds.

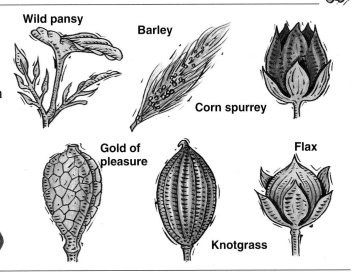

Wild pansy

Barley

Corn spurrey

Gold of pleasure

Flax

Knotgrass

TOOLS FOR THE JOB

Farmers needed the right tools to cultivate their fields. In Europe and Asia they made a variety of special tools to clear the forests. On the left you can see an axe. The cutting part is made from flint (see page 37) which has been ground smooth into a fine cutting edge. The wooden handle and leather thong are modern – part of a museum reconstruction. Experiments have shown that you can cut down a tree about 6 inches in diameter in only seven minutes with this axe! In about 5000 BC in Egypt, farmers used plows pushed by hand, hoes and spades to cultivate the fields beside the River Nile. Most of the fields prehistoric farmers cultivated were small.

ANIMALS

The first farm animals in the world were sheep – around 9000 BC in Iran and Iraq and then goats slightly later, pigs around 7000 BC in Turkey, and cattle around 6000 BC in northern Africa and in the Mediterranean lands. On the right is a herd of soay sheep – a type bred in Europe before the Romans. In other parts of the world different animals were domesticated. In North America it was the turkey, in South America the llama, guinea pig and alpaca, in the European Steppes the horse, and in India the chicken.

DID THEY · HAVE · FAMILIES LIKE · OURS ? ·

Prehistoric peoples lived in families just as we do. How do we know? We have evidence from objects which survive, like these statues. Archaeologists have also excavated the remains of adults and children in prehistoric cemeteries. But we also have the evidence of recording and talking to various prehistoric peoples who have survived into modern times – American Indians, Maoris in New Zealand and Aborigines in Australia, for example.

AN ABORIGINAL FAMILY

For tens of thousands of years, native Australians – the Aborigines – hunted and collected their food. They traveled in groups of about 30 people. In these groups were a few families. An Aboriginal family can be a man with one or more wives and their children. They traveled light, carrying only a few possessions. The hunters and food gatherers would provide for the old and sick in each group.

WHAT DID THEY LOOK LIKE?

Sometimes scientists can reconstruct the faces of ancient people from their skeletons. Sometimes actual pictures or sculptures survive. The two figures above were made from fired clay about 6,000 years ago. The woman (left) and the man (right) were both found in a grave in Romania.

DOING THE WORK

Examples have been found which show prehistoric women, men and children working. This drawing (right) is copied from a real rock painting made about 8,000 years ago in Spain. This painting shows a woman collecting wild honey from a beehive in a tree. She carries a basket to collect the honey which she probably just scooped out with her hands.

Collecting honey

WOMEN IN PREHISTORY

Many archaeologists have assumed that men were more important than women in the past. But there are many examples to show that women were usually as important and often more important than men in prehistory. It was women who:
- provided most of the food in hunting and food gathering groups
- were probably the first to discover how to plant food
- were often rulers in Celtic nations.

CHILDCARE

In hunter-gatherer groups, children were looked after by women as they collected food or they were left with the elderly in camp. This modern Aborigine mother is making a traditional baby's cradle. Dogs, or *dingos*, have been kept as pets and hunters for the last 25,000 years.

· WHERE · · DID · PREHISTORIC · PEOPLE · · LIVE? ·

Have you ever thought that not everyone in the world today lives in a house? Lots of people live in apartments, especially in large cities. But some people today choose to live in mobile homes. Other people are forced to live in tents, such as refugees from wars. What happened in prehistoric times? The first 'houses' were simple shelters built by hunting peoples who had to move about to catch and collect their food. As people discovered how to farm they needed to build permanent places to live in – in villages and then in towns. They learned how to make better constructions – in timber and in stone – and how to heat them in the winter.

MOBILE HOMES

One of the first pieces of evidence for prehistoric houses comes from northern Europe about 12,000 years ago. The great bones of animals such as mammoths were used for the poles of tents. Hides of animals provided the covering. Tent poles were sometimes made from wood when it was available. These early prehistoric 'houses' must have looked a bit like the teepees (right) of these American Indian hunters.

LIVING IN CAVES

Some hunting peoples in Europe and in the Americas lived in caves. Caves could be warm and secure, if you could keep wild animals out! The cave or cliff shelter below is in south-western France and was used by traveling hunters about 12,000 years ago. They probably built walls from wood and animal skins, and made open fires for warmth, cooking and keeping animals away.

There are some extraordinary houses of farming families who lived at a place now called Skara Brae on the Scottish island of Orkney in about 3100 BC. About six houses with walls built of stone were all joined together by covered passageways. The round houses probably had roofs made of wood or whalebone covered with turf and heather.

Here (right) is the inside of one

of those houses from Skara Brae. All the furniture is made from slabs of stone. On the far left is a bed which would have been filled with soft, dry heather. In the center of the room is a hearth for the fire. In front of that (bottom right) is a watertight stone container for keeping shellfish in. Next to it is a grinding stone for barley grain. Around the walls are dressers and built-in cupboards.

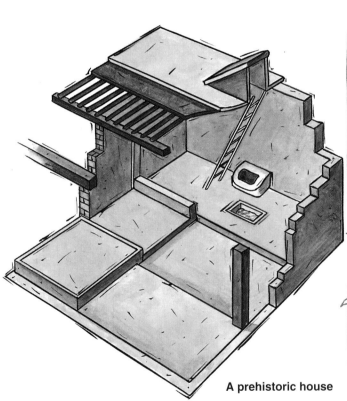

A prehistoric house

A PREHISTORIC TOWN

Prehistoric people could not begin to build towns until there was enough food to support large numbers. Above is a drawing of a house in one of the first farming settlements, at Çatal Hüyük in Turkey. In 7000 BC there was a village here but by 6000 BC it had become a town of about 6,000 people. The houses were all joined together and there were no front doors – you came in through the roof by ladder. Each house had one big room with raised flat areas for sleeping on.

·COULD· PREHISTORIC ·CHILDREN· READ·AND ·WRITE?·

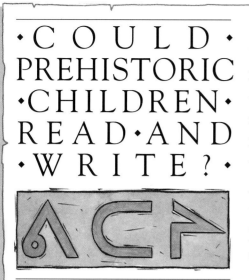

Since this book is about prehistory – the period before writing – you would not expect to find any evidence for reading and writing. Or would you? There is evidence that even people in early prehistoric times used symbols to indicate actions and ideas. Symbols were especially important for rituals and ceremonies. Some of these symbols we do not understand today. Others, like those of the Aborigines of Australia, we can find out about by asking surviving peoples. At the end of the prehistoric period, some peoples began to develop writing. Sometimes it was just a copy of other people's words (see the coin opposite).

ANCIENT RECORDS

This early form of ancient Greek (above) is from the island of Crete. The Greeks from the mainland who conquered Crete around 1450 BC kept records on clay tablets. Some of this ancient writing is in the form of little pictures, pictograms as they are known. The tablets recorded animals, food and equipment in drawings and symbols. Although the written language on clay tablets like this one is still not understood completely, you can see the drawings for chariot wheels quite clearly. An English archaeologist, Sir Arthur Evans, excavated the palace of Knossos on Crete from 1900 and found a great number of these ancient records. He knew that it was ancient writing of some sort but he could not understand it. Experts call this writing Linear B. It was 50 years later that an English scholar, Michael Ventris, deciphered some of this ancient form of writing.

TRADEMARKS

The three seals to the right recorded crates or bales of goods and come from Mohenjo-daro, the earliest city in India. They date from around 2500 BC. The seals probably record the names of merchants. Perhaps the animals shown on the seals are the trademarks of the merchants' companies.

The Inuit had a language, of course, but did not write it down. When people from Europe visited them they started to write down the Inuit's spoken language. Here are two examples:

nanuq is the Inuit word for polar bear.

arlu is orca (killer whale).

The word Inuit means 'the people' but neighboring Indians called them Eskimo, meaning 'eaters of raw flesh'. Travelers from Europe made detailed records of the Inuit peoples and became interested in their languages and dialects (variations of a language). It was the Europeans who gave the Inuit a written alphabet.

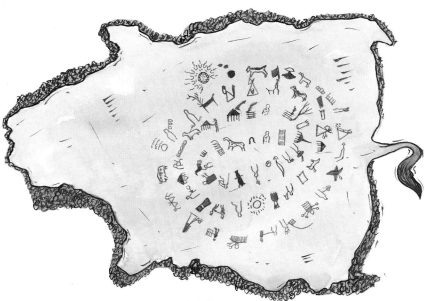

A CALENDAR OF SYMBOLS
This extraordinary object above is a calendar painted onto an animal skin by a Sioux Indian called Lone Dog. He kept the record of his tribe on this skin from 1800 to 1872 – records of wars, diseases and even an eclipse of the sun.

NAMES ON COINS
These two sides of the same coin (above) were made in prehistoric Britain. It is a gold coin of the Celtic king, Cunobelinus, who died just before the Romans invaded Britain in AD 43. The coin uses the Roman written language, Latin. On the left you can see the letters of the king's name (V=U). Above are three letters (AMV) from his capital Camulodunum (now Colchester in eastern England).

·WHAT· ·WORK· ·DID· PREHISTORIC PEOPLE·DO?

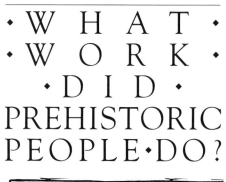

Very few prehistoric people went out to work in the way lots of people do today. Whether you lived in a hunting or a farming group, there were many jobs that needed to be carried out. Most of the things people used had to be made by themselves. Many people became very skillful at making things (see page 36). As groups and communities became bigger, making some things took up so much time that specialists were needed to work at them all the time. In northern Europe, for example, large quantities of flint were needed for tools to clear forests and create fields. Full-time flint miners were needed (see below).

MAORI CLOTHES MAKERS
What are your clothes made of? Cotton, nylon, wool? In prehistoric times, all sorts of materials were used for clothes (see page 24). Below is a full-length Maori cloak made from the fibers of the flax plant. The leaves of the flax were scraped and dried and the fibers twisted into patterns or knotted into strings. This cloak was woven by hand and decorated with lengths of rolled flax fiber which were dyed black.

SPINNING THE THREAD
Tools are the most important pieces of evidence we have for the work prehistoric people did. We know that they were good at inventing things (see page 36). Above you can see a special tool called a spindle. At the end of the wooden spindle is the original round weight made of fired clay. It is called a spindle whorl and this one was used by people in Britain over 2,000 years ago. The clay whorl allows the spindle to turn and spin the wool into a single thread around it. Spindle whorls can be made from stone as well as clay.

DIGGING FOR FLINT...
When prehistoric people began to clear forests at the start of the farming period in northern Europe, they needed lots of flint for axes. Around 3500 BC, the first farmers in Britain soon discovered that flint found on the surface of the ground was not strong enough to make axes. They dug for flint in the ground using deer antler picks (above).

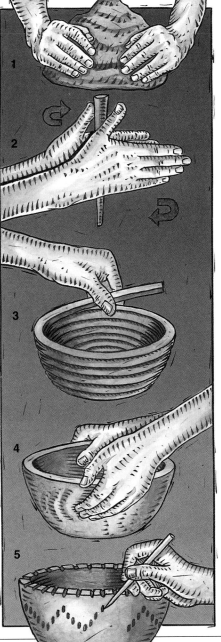

Making objects out of clay was probably invented about 10,000 years ago.

First, clay has to be dug from the ground and worked to make it supple and to remove air bubbles (1).

One type of pottery used by prehistoric people was called coil pottery. They made long sausages of clay and coiled them around to make the shape of the pot (2 and 3).

Then the potter smoothed the sides, inside and out (4).

Prehistoric pots were often decorated (5). Potters used:
twisted cord
cord wound round a stick
fingernails
sharpened wood or bone
combs
animal or bird bones

...UNDERGROUND

This is part of a flint mine in England (right). Miners dug shafts as deep as 40 feet down through soil and chalk. When they found a seam of best quality flint, they dug tunnels like these to get out as much flint as they could. The tunnels had to be quite small so the roof didn't collapse – they left pillars of chalk as props. The iron props you can see are modern.

·WHAT DID· PREHISTORIC ·PEOPLE· ·WEAR?·

Hunting peoples must have made animal skins into clothes. The first farmers discovered how to weave the fibers of plants into cloth – the people of Çatal Hüyük (see page 19) made linen around 6500 BC. American Indians used fibers from the roots of lime and elm trees. Many peoples used bone or wooden needles for sewing. Wild plants were used to dye cloth – yellow from pine cones, green from berries, and brown from onion skins, for example.

JEWELERY

Many prehistoric people all over the world wore jewelery. Sometimes it was simple beads made from shells. But this bracelet (above) is made of seven identical rings of bronze. It comes from France and was made in the Celtic period in the sixth century BC.

COSTUME

On the right is a most elaborate costume worn at a funeral and which was brought back by Captain Cook from Tahiti. The cloth is made from tree bark and is decorated with feathers, pearl shells and coconut shell.

ACCESSORIES

Prehistoric clothes often had to be pinned together. This is a bronze pin, worn by a Celtic man or woman, probably to hold together a cloak. You can see that it is like our modern safety pin but it is elaborate enough to look like a brooch.

Celtic brooch

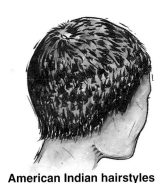

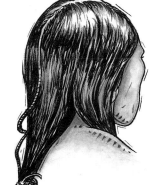

American Indian hairstyles

Danish woman's hairstyle

HAIRSTYLES

Here are drawings of people's hair which has actually survived. The first three from the left are all American Indians from Arizona, preserved in their dry sandy graves from about 1,500 years ago. The last hairstyle (far right) is from a burial in waterlogged peat from prehistoric Denmark. The woman's woolen hairnet has survived.

THE ICE MAN

In 1990, a 5,300-year-old hunter was found preserved in a glacier in the Alps. This is what archaeologists think he looked like from the remains they found. He was carrying a wooden framed back pack and a pouch with flints and tinder for making a fire. His tunic and trousers, made of red deer skin, were lined with straw for warmth. His boots were leather and insulated with straw and birch wood chippings. His hat was made of chamois leather and fur.

Ice man

MUMMIFIED CLOTHES

Mummies do not just come from ancient Egypt! This Inuit baby, who was about six months old, was buried with seven other people around 1475 at Qilakitsoq in Greenland. The baby was wearing a parka and trousers, tied at the waist and ankles. Older Inuit people wore outer and inner trousers and outer and inner boots, called *kamiks*.

·WHO DID· PREHISTORIC ·PEOPLE· ·WORSHIP?·

We know the names of the gods or spirits that surviving prehistoric peoples worship, but we have to use other evidence to find out about ancient prehistoric worship. We know that prehistoric people took great care over burying their dead. They often placed objects in the graves as if the dead person needed them in the world of the dead. Many statues and carvings are found showing worship of some kind. But perhaps the most important evidence comes from the making of special structures, such as the stone circles of Stonehenge.

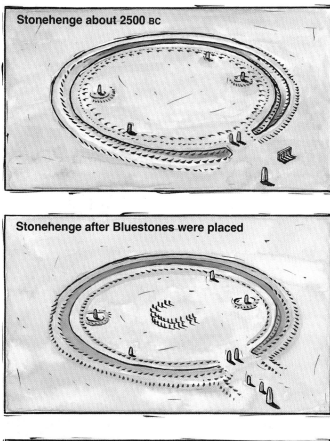

Stonehenge about 2500 BC

Stonehenge after Bluestones were placed

Stonehenge after Sarsen stones replaced Bluestones

STONEHENGE

Stonehenge is probably the most famous stone circle in the world. It was started around 3000 BC. We think it was built as a sort of temple for ceremonies and religious rituals. The positions of the stones and bank were carefully measured out. On midsummer's day the sun rises through the entrance to the monument. An enormous number of people must have helped to build Stonehenge – the biggest stones had to be transported from about 20 miles away. Smaller stones came from Wales over 125 miles away.

ART OR MAGIC?

Hunters in northern Europe painted animals on cave walls. This painting (left) from France shows a bison with arrows and wounds. Some archaeologists think these paintings were magical to bring the hunters success.

MOTHER GODDESS

Many statues like this one (right) from Czechoslovakia have been found from 25,000 BC to 10,000 BC. They are thought to be fertility goddesses, perhaps to encourage births.

EASTER ISLAND STATUES

From about AD 1000 the people of Easter Island, in the Pacific, carved these enormous statues which they called *moai.* Most of the statues are 13 to 16 feet tall with eyes of white coral and painted tattoos on the body. The statues face the sun – perhaps these early Easter Islanders worshiped the sun? Were the statues their gods or their ancestors made into gods?

· D I D · PREHISTORIC · PEOPLE GO · · T O   T H E · · D O C T O R ? ·

You might think that prehistoric people would not be as advanced as we are today in healing and medicine. They did not have hospitals full of machines and instruments, of course. They did go to the doctor, though. We know that they knew about natural cures from plants they gathered. We also know that prehistoric people were able to fix broken bones. They even carried out complicated and dangerous surgery. How do we know all this? You can see some of the archaeological evidence on these pages. We also learn about prehistoric medicine from present-day people, such as the American Indians or the New Zealand Maoris.

SURGERY

This is the skull of an American Indian (left) who lived about 2,000 years ago. His doctor has operated twice, cutting away a small piece of skull bone. The operation was called *trepanation* and was used to cure headaches, skull fractures and epilepsy, and was carried out for magical or religious reasons. The doctor cut out two pieces of skull. We know the second operation (on the right) was not completed – perhaps the man died.

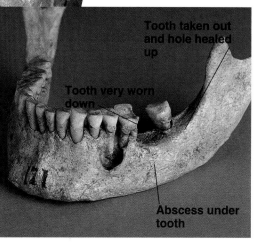

Tooth taken out and hole healed up

Tooth very worn down

Abscess under tooth

GOING TO THE DENTIST

When archaeologists examine skeletons of people, they always look at the teeth. Teeth show how old someone was and what sort of diet they ate. On the right is the lower jaw of someone who lived around 2000 BC in Britain.

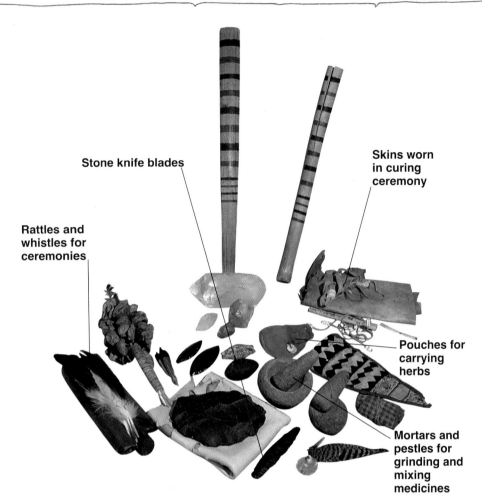

Stone knife blades

Skins worn in curing ceremony

Rattles and whistles for ceremonies

Pouches for carrying herbs

Mortars and pestles for grinding and mixing medicines

MEDICINE MEN AND WOMEN

There were people in North American Indian nations who were skilled in medicine and healing and always had a bundle of tools and supplies. This group (left) belonged to a Miwok healer from California and was used for curing illnesses and for special ceremonies.

NATURAL REMEDIES

Prehistoric whale hunting Indians on the north-west coast of America often used natural cures. Salmonberry bark helped toothache and chewed hemlock poultice stopped bleeding. The farmers at Skara Brae (see page 19) used the plants below:

Henbane for toothache, general aches and to help you sleep

Centaury for healing wounds, eye diseases and an antidote for snake bites

Puff-ball (the inner tissue) to stop bleeding

BURIALS

Excavated skeleton

Archaeologists can discover a lot about prehistoric people when they excavate their skeletons. Careful measurements and records are kept and, if a cemetery is excavated, information about the health and size of a group can often be found. The bones themselves will reveal some of the diseases from which people suffered. For example:

injuries from battle
broken bones which have not healed
arthritis in the joints
leprosy

On the left is the skeleton of someone around thirteen years of age buried with a pot under a mound of earth nearly 4,000 years ago in northern Britain.

·WHO WERE· ·THE· PREHISTORIC ·RULERS?·

Just as there are different types of government and rulers in our modern world, there were different rulers in prehistoric times. Using archaeological evidence and the study of prehistoric peoples who have survived today, we know that there were kings, princes and chieftains. We also know that women as well as men were rulers and leaders in some prehistoric periods. Probably the most famous was Queen Boadicea or Boudica who ruled eastern Britain before the Romans invaded her country, and she led a great uprising against them.

OBJECTS OF POWER

A ruler was someone very powerful in her or his group. We can find evidence for that by looking at the objects which have survived. This beautiful cup (below) is made of a single sheet of beaten gold. Someone very skillful must have been paid to make it. It was found with a skeleton who was buried in Rillaton, south-western Britain around 1500 BC. We do not know the name of this person, but putting such a valuable object into a grave shows that it belonged to someone very important.

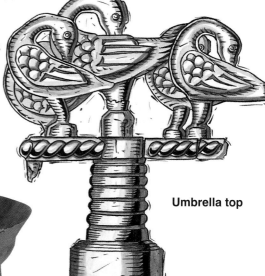

Umbrella top

STATUS SYMBOLS

A status symbol today might be to own a very big car or to build something on your house, such as columns to mark out the front door. We also show what we are like by the clothes we wear and the things we carry around with us. The fancy object above is the top of an umbrella belonging to a king or a chieftain of the Asante people in Ghana, west Africa. Asante was an important kingdom with contact with the Mediterranean world and the East long before Europeans explored there. This was one of the objects brought back to Britain from an

THE FIRST BRITISH QUEEN

A Roman writer described Queen Boudica (left) as 'a very big woman, terrifying to look at, with a fierce look on her face. She had a harsh voice and wore her hair the color of a lion's mane right down to her hips. She used to brandish her spear to strike terror into the hearts of her warriors.'

RULERS TODAY

Think about what our rulers and leaders wear and carry.

Teachers often used to wear a special gown and a hat called a mortar board.

Judges still wear wigs in many countries.

Military commanders wear different uniforms to show their rank. Some of them even carry swords!

Kings and queens wear crowns, elaborate costumes and often carry special objects like the prehistoric mace head below.

BURIED WITH A PRINCE

Archaeologists think that the objects above belonged to a prince who was buried in Britain around 2000 BC. There are bronze daggers, gold ornaments and an axe. The object with a wooden handle and stone end is called a mace head – a status object.

THE SIGN OF A CHIEF

This beautiful object is the war head-dress of a Kiowa chieftain. It is the most important of the status symbols of an American Plains Indian chief. Some Kiowa still live in Oklahoma today.

WERE THERE ·ARTISTS IN· PREHISTORIC ·T I M E S ? ·

All through this book you will see examples of the work of prehistoric artists. They did not paint pictures to hang in art galleries. Their artwork was much more part of their everyday lives. We can work out that many carvings, paintings and craftwork had a special meaning to prehistoric people. We can actually ask some people alive today, the Aborigines of Australia for example, what their art means. We can also say that there were many very skilled prehistoric artists and craftspeople.

ART OR SYMBOLS?

This carving (left) was made in about 3000 BC inside a huge burial mound at Newgrange in Ireland. We do not know what this piece of art meant but we do know something important about the burial monument. On the shortest day of the year (21 December) the rising sun shining directly over the front entrance lights up the burial chamber.

COWBOY BY INDIAN ARTIST

Some prehistoric art records what the artist saw. Here is a good example (right). The Navajo Indians painted a record of what they saw around them in the nineteenth century in Canyon de Chelly in south-western United States of America. In this case the painting shows a strange white-skinned foreigner – a cowboy. The Navajo continued painting on the canyon rocks just as the early inhabitants had done from about AD 1 to about AD 1300.

CHEROKEE CRAFT

This hand-woven basket was made by an American Indian artist from the Cherokee nation in the eighteenth century.

ANCIENT TATTOOS

Some of the most extraordinary remains from the past are tattoos on bodies (right) from graves in Pazyryk in Siberia, Russia. In about 400 BC people were buried here. They were buried in the summer but the ground has remained frozen ever since and therefore has preserved even the skin of their dead bodies.

Tattoos

AFRICAN CAVE ART

In about 6000 BC the Sahara region of Africa had a much wetter climate than it has today. The people who lived around the Tassili caves were cattle farmers. They continued painting the cave shelters (below) as their hunting ancestors had done before them.

MAKE YOUR OWN CAVE PAINTING

The most famous prehistoric art comes from the caves of hunters in south-western France and northern Spain. Above you can see one of the cave walls at Lascaux in France. The artists of this hunting group painted this scene about 15,000 BC. They mixed natural substances to make paint and applied it with sticks, brushes and fingers. Prehistoric artists painted on bumpy walls. You could imitate this by crumpling up a cardboard box, then flattening it out. Paint it with fingers, hands, a stick or home-made brush. Use yellow, red, orange, black and brown paint.

·WHAT DID· ·THEY DO IN· ·THEIR SPARE TIME?·

We know that prehistoric people knew about dancing, music and games. Archaeologists have found examples of musical instruments and paintings which show people dancing. Story-telling was another form of entertainment. It was also an important way of passing on history and traditions to children. Many prehistoric people used dance and music as part of their ceremonies. Surviving hunting peoples (such as the Aborigines) still dance and chant to musical instruments as part of sacred rituals. Can you think of times when other people throughout the world use music in their ceremonies?

DANCING GIRL
This bronze figure is only 4 inches high. She is a dancing girl from the prehistoric Indian town of Mohenjo-daro. The town had about 40,000 people living in it around 2500 BC. The girl is wearing only a necklace and armlets. Perhaps she danced to entertain or as part of a ceremony.

ANIMAL BELLS
Many farmers hang little bells around the necks of their animals. They usually do this so that they can find the animals easily. These bronze bells (below) come from Tanzania in Africa and were hung around a goat's neck. Perhaps prehistoric people also liked the music the bells made.

African animal bells

Lyre or harp

34

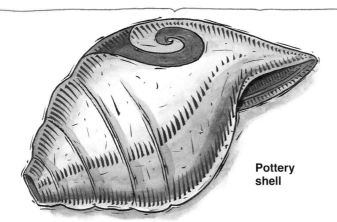

Pottery shell

NOISE FROM SHELLS

Have you ever tried to make noises by blowing into sea shells? Prehistoric peoples the world over used shells to make sounds. The Moche people of Peru even made pottery shells to use as instruments (above) in the first centuries AD.

DEER BONE GAME

Prehistoric peoples often made things from the bones of animals. On the right is a game played by Wailaki American Indians from California. They used counters made out of deer bones.

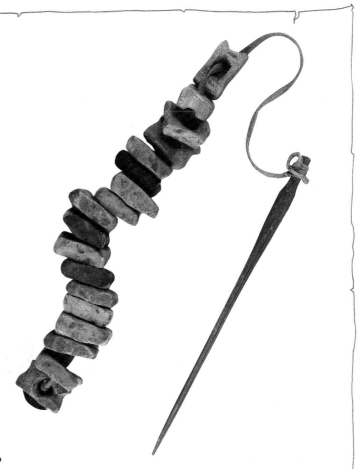

MUSICAL INSTRUMENTS

This lyre or small harp (below) has only survived because it was inside a frozen tomb at Pazyryk in Siberia (see also page 33). It was made in about 400 BC. Part of it has been reconstructed. Its sound box was made of wood with a stretched leather cover. Simpler prehistoric instruments were:

drums, metal rattles, bone flutes, discs with two holes threaded with string which buzzed when twirled.

IRISH HORN

Archaeologists sometimes find metal objects which have been buried for safe keeping. Among these bronze objects, buried nearly 3,000 years ago in Ireland, is a horn. As horns like this have survived, it is possible to hear what they sound like. The horn produces deep, loud notes.

·D I D· PREHISTORIC ·P E O P L E· ·I N V E N T· ·T H I N G S ?·

Many of the things which are familiar to us today were invented a long time ago. One of the things which makes us humans different from animals is our ability to work out solutions to problems – in other words to create inventions. Prehistoric people had to solve all sorts of problems, at first in order to survive, then to make life better. The earliest hunters had to invent tools to kill and cut up their food. The first farmers had to invent tools to cut down forests and break up the soil. Some of the most important inventions by prehistoric people were how to plant seeds for crops, how to tame animals to breed them, the wheel and even early writing.

CLAY POTS
Probably the most important object for anyone – hunter or farmer – was a container. We find them made of all sorts of materials – tree bark, leaves, leather, bone, even stone. About 10,000 years ago people first learned how to make containers from clay which was then made hard by firing (see also page 23). These pots (left) all came from burials in Ireland around 4,000 years ago. You can see that all of them were decorated, at least one of them inside as well as outside.

INVENTING THE WHEEL
Perhaps the most important prehistoric invention of all was the wheel – and we are still using it every day! We think the wheel was invented by people called the Sumerians living over 5,000 years ago in what is now Iraq. The first wheels were solid but about 3,000 years ago spokes were invented. This is a model of a cart from a city in India called Harappa. It was made around 2500 BC. You can still see carts rather like this in parts of the world where tractors and trailers are either too expensive to use or unsuitable for the countryside.

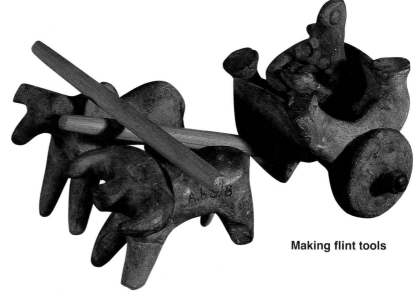

Making flint tools

DISCOVERING METALS

For millions of years people used stone to make tools. Then around 7000 BC they first discovered metal and invented ways of making it into tools. The first metal used was copper which was beaten into shape. Then metalworkers found they could heat it and pour it into molds. The stone mold below was used in Switzerland around 1000 BC to make hair and clothes pins like this one on the right. Gold was also worked into shapes, then bronze and from about 2000 BC, iron was used.

Making things with metal

USING FLINT

Flint is a very hard stone which most prehistoric peoples all over the world used from at least 2.5 million years ago. The first tools were very primitive – flints with sharp broken edges. Soon much better tools were designed, ones that fitted snugly into the palm of a hand and could be used as a heavy knife or axe. The flint needs to be struck by another stone or wood or bone to break off flakes. These flakes can be made into very fine pieces, like the arrowheads below made about 4,000 years ago.

OLD...AND NEW

flint tree axe	chain saw
clay cooking pot	saucepan
bow and arrows	gun
dug-out canoe	motor boat
fishing line	fishing line
(plant fibers)	(nylon)

· D I D · PREHISTORIC · PEOPLE GO · · ON LONG · · JOURNEYS? ·

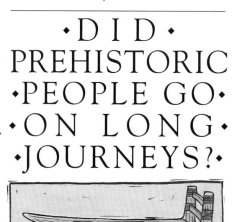

We know prehistoric people made long journeys. If you had to hunt and gather food, you had to follow the animals. If you were a farmer, your nation might have to search to find a good place to settle. Sometimes prehistoric people traveled because they wanted to. People must have traveled a long way to get to Stonehenge. But how did they travel without cars, trains and planes? They built roads and trackways, made boats and ships and, about 6,000 years ago, people in southern Russia learned how to tame the horse. When the wheel was invented, travel became much easier for people across the world.

ANCIENT TRACKWAYS

In the low-lying marshy land in south-western Britain, prehistoric people built trackways of wood from about 3500 BC. This one went for 1.5 miles. These ancient trackways were discovered because peat is dug up here – for burning and for fertilizer.

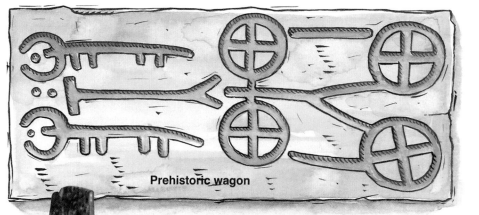

Prehistoric wagon

CARTS AND WAGONS

We know that in some parts of the prehistoric world, people used carts and wagons for transport. You can see a model one from India on page 36. Other peoples made models too, often to put into graves. Above you can see a carving from Sweden made about 2,500 years ago. It looks like a view from above. Can you make out the two oxen with horns, the pulling shaft between them and the four-wheeled wagon behind?

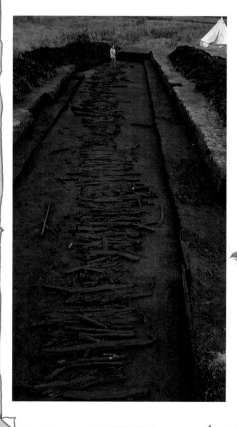

FOLLOWING THE HERDS

Prehistoric hunters had to go where the food was. Many had to travel very long distances tracking animals. On the right you can see a carving on a rock in north-west Russia. The hunter on skis, with a bow and arrow at the ready, is chasing an elk across the ice. Another name for the elk is the moose. The elk is part of the deer family and still lives in northern Europe and in America.

Hunting on skis

TRAVEL BY SEA

Many prehistoric peoples traveled by sea. The first boats were canoes dug out of tree trunks. Sometimes archaeologists find the remains of dug-out canoes. Some prehistoric peoples in the Pacific put two canoes together and sailed vast distances between remote islands – journeys of up to 2,000 miles. The model below is of a canoe of the Maori people of New Zealand. Maori warriors would have filled a full-sized canoe like this to attack their enemies.

ACROSS THE ICE

In Russia, Scandinavia and North America, prehistoric peoples needed to travel across great ice sheets. We know that they had skis (above), snowshoes and sleds. Inuit peoples used sleds to carry heavy loads. This one (below) is made of wood and ivory. Sleds could be dragged by hand, but later Inuits trained teams of dogs to do the pulling.

·DID· PREHISTORIC ·PEOPLE· ·GO TO· ·WAR?·

We do not think that all prehistoric peoples fought wars. When people were hunting and gathering their food there were probably few fights. Then, after the discovery of farming, people started to farm and own land. Disputes, fights and wars began to break out. But how do we know this? Archaeologists find evidence of weapons and armor. They also find towns and villages protected against attack. We know from documents and writing that some prehistoric peoples fought wars. For example, one ancient writer described the Celts – the people the Romans defeated in northern Europe – as 'mad keen on war, full of spirit and quick to begin a fight'.

 ## DEFENDING A PREHISTORIC TOWN

People in Britain started building towns on hilltops in around 700 BC. These Celtic people needed strong defenses to protect themselves from attack. The photograph below is of one of these places, now called Maiden Castle, in southern Britain. Its main defense is a series of huge banks and ditches which enclose an area of 45 acres. From the top of one earth bank to the bottom of the ditch was 46 feet! On top of the banks would have been strong walls, probably made of wood. The entrances to these towns were a sort of maze. Attackers had to pass between high banks inside entrance 'tunnels'. So an enemy could easily be attacked from above.

WEAPONS
Prehistoric peoples invented all sorts of weapons – spears, swords, daggers, for example. The people who lived in Maiden Castle (left) also used sling stones. One store there had over 20,000 pieces of stone ammunition. You can see (above)

AT WAR

We do have some 'pictures' of prehistoric people actually fighting. This beautiful object (below) is a gold comb found in a burial place in southern Russia. It shows a prehistoric people called the Scythians in the fifth century BC. The Scythians were nomads who raised herds of sheep, cattle and horses.

A MAORI DEFENSE

The Maoris of New Zealand built defended settlements like those in Britain. The Maori word for this defense is *pa*. A hilltop was surrounded with ditches and banks of earth. Wooden fences were put up on top of the banks. Maori warriors kept lookout and fought from platforms built on the inside of the fence.

Maori *pa*

an iron dagger and its bronze sheath. It was used by a Celtic warrior in Britain 2,000 years ago. The top of the dagger handle has a human face on it. These Celtic warriors protected their bodies with helmets and shields and often fought from chariots and horses.

·WHAT· HAPPENED ·TO· PREHISTORIC ·PEOPLE?·

Two things happened to prehistoric people. Some simply moved into history! The people in northern Europe, for example, began to use writing when they were occupied by the Romans. When Germany, France and Britain became part of the Roman Empire, those countries stopped being prehistoric. At first the Romans made the written records but later the people themselves began to write. The other thing which happened in some places was that people remained 'prehistoric' until the coming of the Europeans in recent times. This happened in Africa, America, Australia and New Zealand. We know much more about these prehistoric peoples because they were recorded in modern times.

ENDANGERED PEOPLES

Today many peoples are threatened with extinction for lots of reasons. In the past it was often because of invasions from Europe. When the Portuguese arrived in Brazil in the sixteenth century there were 1 to 2 million people. Only about 150,000 survive today – the others were killed by diseases and slavery.

CHANGING PEOPLE

The original peoples of Brazil lived by hunting, fishing and gathering food. Now many people are forced to move because of land development, such as mining and cattle ranching. This Kayapo family (left) try to live their traditional way of life even in the modern world (you can see the watch!).

MAORIS TODAY

The original New Zealanders, the Maoris, arrived there around AD 800. They lived an organized life with complicated customs, laws and ceremonies until 1642 when the first European, Dutchman Abel Tasman, arrived. Maoris still exist today and some of their customs survive. On the left is a Maori woman at the decorated entrance to Whakarewarewa village at Rotorua.

AMERICAN INDIANS

In the nineteenth century, huge numbers of American Indians were killed off by war and disease. They also lost much of their homelands to white settlers. Today about 1.5 million American Indians live on reservations and try to live as their ancestors did. About half of the 300 Indian languages are still spoken.

 ### RECONSTRUCTING THE PAST

One way of keeping prehistory alive is to reconstruct objects, buildings and methods used in the past. This is called experimental archaeology. This reconstruction at Lac de Chalain in France is based on evidence which archaeologists have excavated in a village built by the first farmers. Can you see the trackway running in front of the house?

· GLOSSARY ·

ALPACA Animal tamed in South America and kept mostly for its wool. It looks like a sheep with a long neck.

ARCHAEOLOGY Study of the remains of the past – objects or structures under the ground or sea, on the surface or in standing buildings.

BISON A wild ox often called 'buffalo'.

BRONZE A metal which is a mixture of copper and tin.

CAVE (or ROCK) SHELTERS Used by prehistoric people to camp or settle in. The overhanging cliff also gives protection.

CULTIVATE To prepare the land for growing crops.

DIALECT The word used to describe how people speak a language in a particular area.

DOMESTICATE To tame wild animals and breed them for their meat, milk, wool or skin.

ELK (or MOOSE) A type of large deer which lives in northern Europe and America and which is still hunted today.

EXPERIMENTAL ARCHAEOLOGY Used by archaeologists to try out ideas about what people did in the past and the structures they built.

HOMINID An early form of human.

INSULATE Preventing heat loss – by padding out clothes with other materials for example.

KAMIKS Boots worn by the Inuit people with an inner skin stocking.

KAYAK Canoe used by the Inuit people, made from a wooden frame covered with skins.

LLAMA Large animal tamed by prehistoric South Americans to carry loads.

MAMMOTH Very large animal of the elephant family, now extinct.

MOAI Large statues made by the Easter Island people.

MONUMENT A building or structure that is historically important or interesting.

NOMADS People who move across their territory without making permanent settlements.

PA A defended settlement on a hill – built in New Zealand.

PICTOGRAM The earliest form of writing using pictures.

SETTLEMENT Place where people lived and built their houses.

SLED (or SLEDGE) Wooden construction used by people to pull loads over snow and ice. Can be pulled by animals (often dogs) or by people.

SORGHUM A kind of grass collected and grown to eat.

STONE CIRCLE Built by prehistoric peoples as part of their worship or ceremonies. Large stones were placed upright in the ground.

TAPIR A short powerful animal found in South America.

TREPANATION Surgery which involved cutting a small piece from the top of the skull to expose the brain.

◆ I N D E X ◆